W9-BQU-029

A GIFT OF

2003

THE G. I. SERIES

General George Patton wearing his fourth star for the first time in April 1945. He is wearing a privately tailored 'Ike' jacket. On his highly polished helmet liner are the four stars of his rank, as well as the Third Army insignia and the divisional insignia of the 1st and 2d Armored Divisions. The thickness of the brim on this liner indicates that it is the early pattern papier-mâché liner, and not the later model fibre liner. (SCAPA)

THE G. I. SERIES

THE ILLUSTRATED HISTORY OF THE AMERICAN SOLDIER, HIS UNIFORM AND HIS EQUIPMENT

Patton's Third Army

Christopher J. Anderson

CHELSEA HOUSE PUBLISHERS
PHILADELPHIA

Library of Congress Cataloging-in-Publication Data
Anderson, Christopher J.
Patton's Third Army / Christopher J. Anderson
   p. cm.—(The G.I. series)
Originally published: London: Greenhill Books; Mechanicsburg, Pa.: Stackpole Books, ©1997.
Includes index.
Summary: Focuses on the uniforms and equipment of the Third Army while describing its movement across Europe during World War II.
ISBN 0-7910-5374-1
1. United States. Army. Army, 3rd—History Pictorial works.   2. World War, 1939–1945—Regimental histories—United States Pictorial works.   3. World War, 1939–1945—Campaigns—Western Front Pictorial works   [1. United States. Army. Army, 3rd—Uniforms—History.   2. United States. Army. Army, 3rd—Equipment—History.   3. World War, 1939–1945—Campaigns.]   I. Title.   II. Title: Patton's 3rd Army. III. Series: G.I. series (Philadelphia, Pa.)
D769.26 3RD.A55   1999
940.54'21'0222—dc21   99-20139
                         CIP

ACKNOWLEDGEMENTS

I would like to thank Mr. Robert Melhorn, U.S. Army Public Affairs, the National Archives, Dr. John Langellie and the Historical Society of the Militia and National Guard for their help in obtaining photographs. I would also like to thank all of the veterans of the Third Army whom I have pestered over the years for their memories.

ABBREVIATIONS

SCAPA	Signal Corps Army Public Affairs
SCHSM & NG	Signal Corps, Historical Society of the Militia and National Guard
SCNA	Signal Corps National Archives
SCA	Signal Corps Authors Collection

Designed and edited by DAG Publications Ltd
Designed by David Gibbons
Layout by Anthony A. Evans
Printed in Hong Kong

PATTON'S THIRD ARMY

6 July 1944, a month after the Allied landings
France, Lieutenant General George S. Patton
d a small advance party arrived in Nehou,
nce, to establish 'Lucky Forward', the Third
my's first headquarters in Europe. Through
y, while the Allies struggled to break out of the
lemate in the hedgerows of Normandy, thou-
ids of troops who would become the Third
my, began to assemble.

On 1 August 1944, the Third Army began its
st full day of operations in support of Opera-
n COBRA, the Allied effort to break out of Nor-
undy. Patton was directed to advance to the
uth and clear the Brittany Peninsula and its
rts, vital to the enemy. The Third's advance
vards Brest and Lorient was undertaken with
:redible speed, the 6th Armored Division
vancing 150 miles in one week. By the end of
gust, not only had the Third Army cleared the
ttany Peninsula of the majority of German
·ces, but it had also turned east and closed the
uthern flank of the Falaise Gap at Argentan.

Patton continued to advance east after the
:akout from Normandy. The advance of the
ird and the other Allied armies was so rapid
it supplies, particularly petrol, were a scarce
mmodity. In early September 1944, the deci-
n was made to divert all petrol supplies to
ntgomery's 21st Army Group in support of
eration MARKET GARDEN. This necessitated a
lt in the Third's advance. Patton was impatient
th this delay, believing that this allowed the
rmans, who had been retreating up to this
int, time to consolidate their positions east of
e Rhine. During September and October 1944,
lited advances were made and the Third con-
lidated its position and began its effort to
Juce the fortress city of Metz.

The summer and early autumn of 1944 saw the
ird Army race across France and begin to nib-
ble at the edges of the Siegfried Line. By October
and November, the Third Army was a victim of
its own success. General Eisenhower simply
could not keep Patton's tanks full of petrol and
the Third was forced to stop.

Throughout the summer of 1944, when the
Third was taking France by storm, Patton's men
wore 18 oz olive drab (OD) wool serge trousers
and the OD wool flannel shirt. The shirt featured a button-over placket at the neck and
wrist that was designed to assist the shirt's
'anti-gas' properties. In many cases, soldiers
removed these extra pieces of material because
they caused chafing. The wool trousers and
shirt were worn over cotton or wool underwear.
By 1944, most undergarments issued were olive
drab, although there was still occasional use of
the earlier white underwear. Over the wool shirt,
most men would have worn the OD cotton
M1941 field jacket. This lightweight jacket was
lined with shirt-weight wool and had been the
standard field jacket since the beginning of the
war.

Members of armoured units, and a small number of infantrymen, wore the winter combat
jacket and trousers. The winter combat jacket,
more commonly referred to as the 'tanker's
jacket', was a cotton jacket lined with a blanket-
weight wool kersey. The winter combat trousers
were bib fronted and constructed of the same
materials as the jacket. The jacket featured knitted cuffs and collars and was closed with a zip.
This jacket was coveted by the G.I.s in the Third
as it was the most comfortable and stylish one
available to them.

Insignia of rank, as well as divisional insignia,
were sewn to both the M1941 and the winter
combat jackets. Insignia were worn on both
sleeves and the divisional or army patch on the
left shoulder. However, insignia were often

removed from jackets to hide unit identity and the wearer's rank while in the field.

Some men also wore the herringbone twill (HBT) jacket and trousers. During the Third's advance, HBTs were largely confined to rear-echelon and specialist troops. However, armoured unit soldiers and some infantry and artillery personnel did wear this clothing, either as a warm weather uniform or a supplementary layer of clothing during the winter.

At the beginning of Patton's campaign, the standard footwear was the reverse upper service shoe, better known as the 'rough-out' boot. It was constructed with the rough side of the leather out and had rubber soles. Many Europeans recall that they could always tell that it was Americans marching by because the sound made by their rubber-soled shoes was so different from the hobnailed boots worn by all other European armies. It was believed that constructing a shoe with the rough side of the leather out would improve comfort for the wearer and make the application of waterproofing to the outside of the shoe easier. The 'rough-out' boot quickly replaced the standard service shoe for troops serving overseas. To protect his legs, a soldier wore M1938 canvas leggings. The trousers were tucked into the leggings for added protection and neatness.

By the time the Third found itself halted before Metz, many men had begun to receive the two-buckle combat boot in lieu of the service shoe. The two-buckle boot was the same as the service shoe, except that a leather top was added to the boot to eliminate the need for leggings.

Ballistic protection for the head was provided by the M1 steel helmet. This helmet, designed to replace the earlier M1917A1 helmet, was constructed of a steel shell and fibre liner. The size of the liner could be adjusted to fit the head. A variety of helmet nets were issued, or improvised, to break up the silhouette of the helmet, attach camouflage and prevent a sheen to the helmet when wet. When the liner was removed, the shell was utilized for a variety of things from wash-basin to cooking pot. Underneath the helmet the soldier often wore the woollen 'beanie' cap. This cap, hated by senior officers, was designed with a peak at the front to keep the helmet from sliding over the eyes of the wearer. It was not intended to be worn as an item of headgear on its own but frequently was.

The men of the Third wore a variety of cott webbing equipment over their uniforms. Ri men wore the 10-pocket M1923 cartridge b designed to hold 80 rounds of ammunition, w additional ammunition being carried in disp able cotton bandoliers slung over the shoulde A canteen and first aid kit were also attached this belt, which was then attached to the M19 haversack. The haversack was designed to su port the weight of the ammunition belt and ho the soldier's shelter half, blanket and mess-ge A bayonet and entrenching tool, either the handle shovel or the later folding shovel, we also attached to the haversack. The M1928 hav sack was designed to carry only specific ite and was loathed by men in the field. Some s diers discarded their haversacks and support the weight of their equipment with the M19 combat suspenders. Their personal items we carried in the M1936 musette bag attached to t suspenders. None of the systems designed support a soldier's equipment proved entire effective, and many men made a bed-roll out their blankets and slung it over their shoulder

Tankers, and other soldiers who did r require a heavy load of equipment, wore t M1936 web pistol belt. They attached pouch designed to carry ammunition for either the . calibre pistol or .30 calibre carbine to the be The pistol was worn in a holster that was eith attached to the pistol belt or worn as a shoulc holster. In addition, the Army also issued a va ety of specialised webbing equipment, such those items issued to medics.

The standard firearm of the Third Army s dier was the .30 calibre M1 'Garand' rifle. T Garand, called by Patton, 'The greatest bat implement ever devised', was a 9.5 lb, eight-sh semi-automatic rifle. Officers, and those m whose primary job was not that of a riflem were authorised to use the .30 calibre, semi-au matic, M1 carbine. This weapon was lighter th the Garand, but had substantially less range a hitting power and was not favoured by ma troops. A variety of automatic weapons, such the Browning Automatic Rifle (BAR), the .45 ca bre Thompson and M1917A1 .30 calibre machi gun, provided additional fire support to t infantry. Tankers generally favoured the light M3A1 .45 calibre machine gun and the M1911 . calibre pistol.

For greater firepower, infantry units would supported by the 60mm and 81mm morta zookas and 57mm anti-tank guns assigned to ch battalion. Armoured battalions would be pported by bazookas and M3 halftracks carry- g 81mm mortars.

Soldiers were members of one of the 26 antry or 12 armoured divisions that served, varying lengths of time, with the Third Army m August 1944 until the end of the war. In dition to the infantry and armoured divisions, ere were a variety of specialised units assigned the Third.

The armoured division comprised, at full ength, of 10,900 men. Some of these men nned the division's 263 tanks, the majority ing M4 Shermans. Personnel were also signed to the division's attached artillery regi- nts, armed with self-propelled 105mm how- ers, armoured infantry battalions or other ached units. The armoured element in each ision was divided into three tank battalions, ch with 53 Sherman tanks; three armoured antry battalions, each with approximately 00 men; and three divisional artillery battal- s each with 54 105mm howitzers.

The second component of the Third Army was e infantry division. Each infantry division cluded approximately 14,000 men. These men re divided among the division's three infantry giments, each made up of 3,000 men, three tillery regiments, armed with 105mm how- ers and 155mm howitzers, and attached per- nnel.

After being stalled during October 1944, the ird continued its advance eastwards. By 18 vember, Metz had been completely isolated. ile elements of the Third contained the city, e remainder of the Army continued advancing stwards and reached the Saar river, on the Ger- n border, at the beginning of December.

Metz fell in early December. With the majority the Third Army at the edge of the Siegfried e, the assault on the Siegfried Line was sched- ed for 19 December. Despite the initial delays used by lack of fuel, determined German resis- ce at Metz and the worsening weather of late tumn and early winter, the Saar campaign had ccessfully brought the Third Army to the Ger- n border.

With the arrival of inclement weather during e Saar campaign, soldiers began to wear arctic ershoes or shoe-pacs. The arctic overshoe was signed to be worn over the field shoe. Initially nufactured entirely of rubber, the overshoe

was later changed to a rubber bottom and canvas upper to conserve scarce rubber supplies. The shoe-pacs were designed to be worn instead of the combat boot. These were made of rubber soles and leather uppers.

Also making its appearance during the Saar campaign was the 32 oz wool overcoat. The over- coat's weight and length made it very unpopular with front-line soldiers as it restricted move- ment. In place of the overcoat, some men wore the mackinaw or arctic field jacket. Both of these cotton jackets were lined with blanket-weight wool and were shorter than the overcoat. How- ever, due to the limited availability of the macki- naw and the arctic field jackets, and the weight of the overcoat, many men just wore the five-button sweater, under their field jacket, or did without.

In addition to various items of cold weather clothing worn during the late autumn of 1944, new items of clothing and equipment began to arrive in the various units of the Third Army. Among the new items were the M1943 field jacket and trousers. This field jacket was designed to replace the M1941 field jacket. Com- plaints from the field about the M1941 field jacket indicated that it was too light for cold weather and too heavy for warm weather. The new jacket was made of water-repellent cotton and was designed to be worn over several layers of clothing. Trousers were also developed for use with the new jacket, but these were not worn as often.

However, the new M1943 uniform did not entirely replace the older uniforms. Delays in production and delivery ensured that all types of uniforms were seen until the end of the war. It was very common for divisions arriving from the United States after the initial campaigns in Nor- mandy to be completely outfitted in the newer M1943 clothing before departing for Europe. Sol- diers in divisions that had been in Europe for some time continued to wear the earlier uniform and made the change over to the M1943 jacket much more sporadically. Equipped with a mix- ture of uniforms, the men of the Third Army pre- pared for their greatest battle.

The planned advances against the Siegfried Line were changed quickly on 16 December when the Germans, in an attempt to halt the advance of the Allied forces in the west, launched the Ardennes offensive. German armies, under Field Marshal von Rundstedt, made rapid progress against elements of the American First Army and surrounded the American garrison of the critical road junction of Bastogne.

The situation was serious as Allied generals met to discuss how they could contain the German advance. Patton stunned the audience when he announced that he could halt the advance of the Third Army eastwards, turn it 90 degrees to the north and attack the southern flank of the German advance in three days. Patton explained that he was able to do this because his staff, alerted to events in the north, had prepared for this eventuality while they were advancing to the east.

Four days later, the 4th Armored, 26th, 35th, 80th and elements of the 28th Infantry Divisions pushed north to relieve the besieged garrison of Bastogne. Despite the rapid change of direction and appalling weather conditions, the Third advanced northwards. On the afternoon of 26 December, the 37th Tank Battalion, 4th Armored Division, commanded by future chief of staff of the Army, Colonel Creighton Abrams, broke through to Bastogne. For the remainder of December and the first part of January 1945, the Third Army, continued to tear into the southern shoulder of the German bulge. By 15 January it had linked up with elements of the First Army at Houffalize. The Battle of the Bulge was successfully concluded due, in large part, to the efforts of the Third Army.

After closing off the German advance in January, the Third Army returned to the positions it had held prior to the start of the battle and continued its advance eastwards. By 13 March, 1945, the Third had advanced through the Siegfried Line and arrived on the west bank of the Rhine.

Fearing that the planned crossing of the Rhine by Montgomery's 21st Army Group would halt his advance, as it had done in September, Patton was determined to cross the Rhine before Montgomery.

On 22 March, two days before General Montgomery's scheduled crossing, Major General Manton Eddy, XII Corps Commander, was able to get elements of the 5th Infantry Division over the Rhine by using the Third Army's L4 spotter planes to ferry men across the river. By 23 January, engineers had constructed a bridge and the entire 5th Infantry Division was across.

After crossing the Rhine, the Third continued its rapid advance through southern Germany, ending its war in Plzen, Czechoslovakia.

During the nine months and eight days in which the Third Army conducted active operations in Europe, it was credited with the liberation of more than 118,000 square miles of territory and 12,000 cities and towns and was inflicting nearly one-and-a-half million casualties on the German Army. German generals rightly came to fear the Third Army as the best that the Allies had. Yet, despite these awesome statistics, the men who served in the Third Army were different from the millions of other American soldiers in terms of uniforms, equipment organisation. It was the dynamic leadership of George S. Patton that enabled the soldiers of the Third Army to advance further and faster than any other American Army during World War II. Today it is with a justifiable pride in their accomplishments that the veterans of the Third Army still boast that during the war 'I rolled with Georgie'.

The Photographs

Every attempt has been made to only use photographs of members of the Third Army. However, original captions for many of the photographs are incorrect or missing altogether. Whenever possible, unit identification has been listed with each picture. In all cases, the equipment being worn by soldiers in these pictures would have been used by members of the Third Army during the campaign in Europe.

Bibliography

Armed Forces Quartermaster Supply Catalog U.S. Government 1943 (reprinted by George A. Peterson, National Capital Historical Sales).

The Armies of George S. Patton, George Forty (Arms and Armour, 1996).

Doughboy to GI, Kenneth Lewis (Norman D. Larsing Publishing, 1993).

QMC Historical Studies, The Development of Special Rations for the Army, U.S. Government, 19 (reprinted by George A. Peterson, National Capital Historical Sales).

Uniforms, Weapons and Equipment of the World War II GI, Stephen Sylvia and Michael O'Donnell (Moss Publications, 1982).

When The Third Cracked Europe, General Paul Harkins (Army Times Publishing Company, 1969).

World War II GI in Color Photographs, Richard Windrow and Tim Hawkins (Windrow and Greene, 1993).

World War II Order of Battle, Shelby Stanton (Galahad Books, 1984).

An infantry sergeant stands at Sling Arms. This sergeant is wearing the wool shirt and trousers that were the standard combat uniform of Patton's Third Army, as well as of other G.I.s. He is wearing the Garand belt and M1928 haversack. He has attached his bayonet to the left side of his belt. Usually, when the pack was worn, the bayonet was attached to the left side of the haversack. The sergeant has also attached a grenade pouch to his right leg. This pouch was attached to the Garand belt and then secured to the leg by an integral web tape around the thigh. (SCNA)

Left: A 5th Armored Division tank crew load rounds for their tank's 75mm gun. All four of the men are wearing herringbone twill (HBT) coveralls, winter combat (tanker's) jacket and armoured forces' crew helmet. The cords that are draped over the left shoulders of the two men on the ground carry jacks for the headset. The cord would be plugged in to the tank's intercom system so that the men could communicate. Three of these men have sewn the 5th Armored Division patch to their left shoulders. (SCNA)

Left: A soldier of the 5th Armored Division takes a message during a training exercise early in the war. The soldier is wearing the one piece HBT uniform over a white T-shirt. On his left side he has attached an M1 gas mask. He has sewn his divisional insignia on to the left hand side of his chest. The 5th Armored Division would arrive in France in July of 1944. After a short time with the Third Army, the division would be transferred to the First Army. (SCNA)

ht: Engineer soldiers train
or to their deployment in
ope. They are wearing the
l uniform with M41 field jack-
Of special interest are the toe-
ped service shoes being worn
er the leggings. These shoes,
ch featured a smooth outside
face and toe-cap, would have
n replaced in the ETO by the
e common rough-out service
es. The rough-out service
es would have featured the
gh side of the leather on the
side of the shoe and no toe-
. (SCNA)

ow: Three soldiers prepare
od plasma for delivery to the
opean Theater of Operations
O). The knowledge that men
ld be well cared for if wound-
was crucial to morale. The sol-
r on the left is wearing the
ndard wool uniform and over-
s cap. The men in the centre
l on the right are wearing the
ton herringbone twill (HBT)
gue uniform. The man in the
tre has buttoned over the gas
o of his HBT shirt, while the
n on the right is wearing a
te cotton T-shirt.. (SCNA)

Above: A forward artillery obser
with a field phone and radio,
directs his battery's artillery
rounds. Infantry units would hav
observers from artillery units
attached to direct artillery fire.
Artillery support was a crucial el
ment in the Third Army's succes.
On the left of the picture are sev
al boxes of K rations. These ratio
were the most frequently consumed ration on the frontline. Ea
box contained a complete meal.
Boxes were marked separately fo
breakfast, lunch and dinner. (SCN

Left: A private first class of the
87th Infantry Division prepares t
enjoy some beer and pretzels. He
wearing the flannel shirt. On his
helmet liner he has attached a
decal of rank below his divisiona
insignia. Just visible on his right
wrist is a privately purchased na
bracelet. These bracelets, from
loved ones at home or acquired a
many post exchanges (PX), were
popular items with G.I.s. As well
being decorative, they served as
additional means of identification
should the soldier be killed or
wounded. (SCNA)

ht: Engineer soldiers train on the struction of a pontoon bridge. se men are all wearing the wool sers and shirt with field jackets. man in the centre is wearing the t pattern 'Olive Drab Field Jacket', nmonly known as the M1941. This ket differed from the later, and re common, M41 field jacket only he pockets. Pockets on the M38 ket featured a button closure flap r the pocket. This was eliminated m the M41 field jacket. (SCNA)

ow: A group of Third Army men waiting to be transported over the er Rhine. The man sitting in the eground is wearing the standard ol shirt and trousers and M1941 d jacket. He has a privately uired red bandanna around his k to reduce chafing. This bandan-would probably have been moved closer to the front line, as its ght colour could expose the wearer nnecessary attention. Around his st, the man is wearing a navy life-server. This life-preserver could be ated with either two CO_2 catridges he front of the belt or manually. ny veterans of the Normandy land-s complained that when these life-ts were inflated, they caused the arer to flip upside down. (SCNA)

t: An M4A1 Sherman tank unloads from a Landing
ɔ Tank (LST) in France. These vessels could carry a
ɔber of the M4 Sherman tanks, or a variety of other
sonnel and equipment. Landing vehicles such as
se were crucial to the invasion and, later, the build-
and breakout in France. The tank is obviously new
he theatre. Soon the crew of this tank will have fes-
ned their vehicle with a variety of things to improve
ir living conditions and chances of survival. (SCNA)

ɔve: At the end of the war in Europe, gunners of the
h Infantry Division prepare their M2A1 105mm
ʋitzers for shipment back to the United States. The
mm was the standard field piece of American
ɪntry divisions during the war in Europe. Each
ɪntry division would have been equipped with 36 of
se guns. In armoured divisions, the 105mm was
ɪnted on a Sherman tank chassis and operated as
-propelled artillery. At the left of the picture are the
-and-a-half-ton trucks that towed the 105mms.
NA)

ht: A soldier boards the ship that will take him
ne. Over the wool trousers and shirt this man has
ɪg the three-snap gas mask bag, most likely being
d as a haversack. Over his shoulders are the straps
the M1944 combat pack. This pack system, inspired
he Marine Corps' 782 gear, did not arrive in the
ɔpean Theatre until very late in the war and was
often seen in use. The two straps across his chest
probably for the M1936 musette bag. Normally, the
hooks at the end of the straps would be hooked to
ngs on the M1936 combat suspenders. (SCNA)

Above: In a staged photograph, tw
III Corps MPs guard a bridge over
Rhine. Both men wear the cotton
M1943 field jacket with wool shir
and trousers. They are also wearin
two-buckle combat boots. Both me
have white MP designation painte
on their helmets. The MPs are bot
armed with .30 calibre carbines ar
carry extra magazines in a pouch
attached to the right of their pistc
belts. The flag on the right, and th
shield at their feet, are the design
tion for the III Corps. The III Corp
was part of the Third Army from
October 1944 to February 1945 ar
again at the end of the war. (SCNA

Left: At the war's end, three veter.
of the Third Army talk with a Swi
watchmaker during a leave. All th
men are wearing wool 'Eisenhowe.
jackets, wool trousers and two-
buckle boots. The 'Eisenhower'
jacket was inspired by the British
battledress and ETO jackets. It ha
been originally designed to be wo
as a liner to the M43 field jacket b
was instead used as a dress, or Cl.
A, jacket. The man on the right ha
sewn a Third Army patch to his le
shoulder. He is also wearing a late
pattern trouser with a pocket flap
added to the back pockets. Earlier
patterns of trouser would would
have had a simple slash pocket.
(SCNA)

Above: Technician 5th Grade Jack Hutton, a Signal Corps photographer, takes shots in the ruined town of St Vith, Belgium, after severe fighting. Hutton wears wool trousers, leggings and field jacket. He has modified the M1916 leather holster by removing its leather flap. Just visible inside the holster is an M1911A1 .45 calibre pistol, the standard pistol of the American armed forces during the war. He is taking his pictures with a Bell & Howell 16mm camera. Signal Corps' photographers took some of the most famous pictures of the war, being present at the front lines for much of the time and have left a lasting record of the contributions of the G.I.s. (SCAPA)

Left: At war's end, Patton prepares to skipper a small pleasure craft captured by the men of the Third Army. He is wearing a privately tailored 'Ike' jacket and 'pink' jodhpurs. The pistol was one of many that Patton wore during the war, not all of which had ivory handles. Patton did not wear these weapons merely as ornamentation – he was an accomplished pistol marksman. (SCAPA)

Above: In October 1944 General Patton takes time out to load more film into his camera. He is standing behind his specially modified jeep. The jeep featured sirens mounted on the hood. Patton would have his driver blare these sirens to announce his arrival during his many inspection tours. Also visible on the hood of the jeep are the Third Army pennant and Patton's lieutenant general's flag. (SCAPA)

ht: General Patton rides the
se 'Favory Africa'. This
se had been picked by
lf Hitler as a gift for
eror Hirohito of Japan.
horse was captured as the
rd Army advanced into
tria. General Patton's Third
y insignia and rank are
ble on his left shoulder. On
highly polished helmet
r are the insignia for the
nth Army and the II
ps. Patton had commanded
II Corps in North Africa
Sicily. The thickness of the
net liner would indicate
t this is the earlier papier-
hé model. (SCAPA)

posite page, bottom: General Dwight D. Eisenhower,
reme Allied Commander (left), is greeted by General
rge Patton. General Omar Bradley, Commander 12th Army
up (far right), and Lieutenant General Courtney Hodges,
mander First Army, look on. Generals Eisenhower and
ton are both wearing privately purchased 'Ike' jackets,
nhower with trousers and Patton with jodhpurs. Of spe-
interest is Eisenhower's rank insignia, visible on his right
ulder. General Bradley wears an issue 'Ike' jacket with
atrooper boots. General Hodges is wearing an Army Air
ce B-14 flight jacket. On the left shoulder of General
dges' jacket is the First Army patch. Generals Bradley and
dges have green cloth strips on their jacket epaulets identi-
g them as combat commanders.

Above: In November 1944, Mr Averill Harriman (centre)
American Ambassador to the Soviet Union, tours the front
with Lieutenant General George Patton. Patton is wearing an
officer's trench coat over an Army Air Force B-10 or B-15
jacket, identified by the fake fur collar. He has sewn the
Third Army patch to the left shoulder of his trench coat. The
three men are travelling in Patton's personal armoured car.
The armoured car has been modified by the attachment of a
Third Army flag, as well as a lieutenant general's three star
flag and plate. Patton further modified this vehicle with the
addition of a windscreen and horns. (SCAPA)

General Patton, centre, stands with his officers and his dog 'Willie' in September 1944. Patton wears two-buckle boots w
his tailored 'Eisenhower' jacket and general officers' pistol belt. Standing at the right, in the foreground, Major Genera
Walton Walker, Commander of XX Corps, wears leather legging topped boots originally designed for the cavalry and a
privately tailored ETO jacket. (SCAPA)

...t: The four generals
...erring over the relief
...del are, from left to right,
...eral Patton, Major General
...ton Walker (XX Corps),
...or General S. Leroy Irvin
... Infantry Division) and
...eral George Marshall.
...y wear a variety of
...orms. Generals Patton
... Marshall both wear the
...on trench coat while
...eral Walker wears a
...ately tailored ETO jacket
... a non-regulation leather
... and .45 pistol holster.
...eral Irvin wears a winter
...bat jacket to which he
... added Army Air Force
...her general's rank and
...her name tag. The leather
...gnia was originally intend-
...or use on leather flying
...kets, but it was not unusu-
... see it worn on the cloth-
...of senior officers. (SCAPA)

...ht: General Patton pins a
...er Star on Private Ernest
...enkins. Jenkins was
...rded the Silver Star for
... participation in the cap-
...e of 15 German soldiers at
...teaudun, France, in 1944.
...kins, a quartermaster
...ps soldier, was a member
... he famed 'Red Ball
...ress'. Jenkins is wearing
... standard wool shirt and
...users and is armed with
...M1903A3 rifle. This rifle,
...ginally used during World
...r I, had largely been
...laced by the M1 Garand
... 1944, but could still be
...nd in some rear-echelon
...ts. This photograph also
...vides a good view of one
...Patton's trademark ivory
...dled pistols, in this case a
...t 44/45 single action.
...APA)

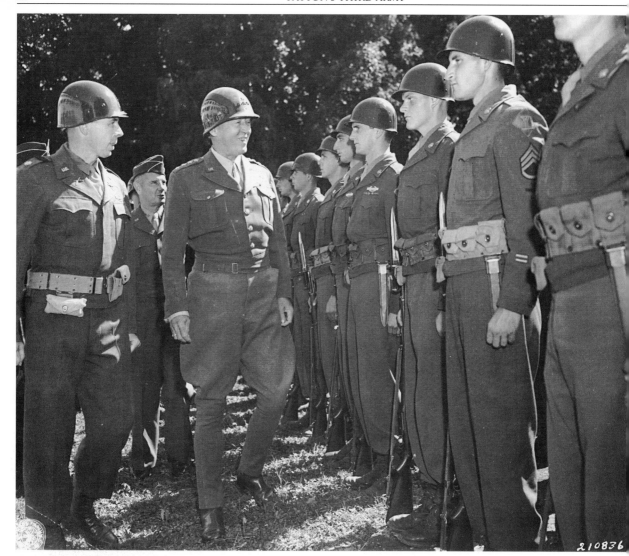

210836

osite page, top: General Patton
ews the 2nd Battalion, 328th
ntry Regiment, 26th Infantry
sion. Patton is wearing his privately
red 'Ike' jacket and jodhpurs. The
a are all wearing issue 'Ike' jackets
highly polished helmet liners. The
patch of the 26th Division can be
on the left shoulders of the men.
letters YD stood for 'Yankee
sion', the division's nickname. Also
e the Combat Infantry Badge being
n by the men standing fourth and
a from the left. (SCHSM & NG)

osite page, bottom: General Patton
gratulates soldiers of the XX Corps
their efforts in France in November
4. The men standing around Patton
wearing a variety of field jackets. Of
cial interest is the soldier standing in
centre foreground who is wearing
'Ike' jacket. This jacket, although
nded to be worn as a liner to the
043 field jacket, was seldom worn in
field. Major General Walton H.
ker, the commander of the XX Corps,
ading on Patton's left, is wearing an
ny Air Force B-10 jacket. (SCHSM &

ve right: Major General Willard S.
l, commanding general, 26th
ntry Division. The 26th was a
ional Guard unit from New England.
as the first American combat divi-
a to be sent directly from the United
es to France after the invasion.
eral Paul wears an M43 field jacket
n embroidered rank insignia on the
ulets. He is wearing standard issue
-buckle combat boots. He wears
e horsehide riding gloves to protect
hands. Just visible on his right
ulder is the strap to his leather .45
ulder holster. (SCHSM & NG)

ht: Brigadier General Cota presents
t Sergeant Sam Pizzo with the silver
. Sergeant Pizzo wears what
ears to be a recently issued arctic
l jacket. Although these jackets
e considered obsolete by 1944,
usands of them were shipped to
ope to make up for a shortage of
l weather clothing. Pizzo has also
iaged to obtain a pair of para-
per jump boots. These highly cov-
l boots were not normally issued to
soldiers. (SCHSM & NG)

Above: Brigadier General Norman Cota pins the Silver Star onto Captain Paul F. Gaynor. General Cota is wearing the winter combat jacket, to which he has attached his insignia of rank. On the back of his helmet is a vertical stripe used as a means of identification on officers' helmets. Non-commissioned officers' helmets would have featured a horizontal stripe. Captain Gaynor is wearing an M1943 field jacket. His divisional patch and captain's insignia have been attached to the coat. This insignia would, most likely, have been removed by Gaynor once he returned to the front lines. (SCHSM & NG)

Above: Major General Paul Baade presents Private Buste Brown with the Distinguished Service Cross. General Ba is wearing a British-made officer's field overcoat. He ha camouflage scarf around his neck. Private Brown is wea the second pattern mackinaw. This was identical to the pattern except that the collar was now cotton, whereas first pattern had a blanket wool collar. Private Brown ha M3 fighting knife in the later war M8 scabbard attached his pistol belt. (SCHSM & NG)

Left: Major Gener Norman Cota, 28 Division comman shares a package home with Sergea Joseph Bunch. Ge Cota is wearing th M1943 field jacke liner. Next to hot mail was the mos important elemen maintaining the morale of the sol Every effort was r to ensure that ma was delivered in a timely fashion. Sergeant Bunch h received cookies, pecans and a pen pencil set in his p age. Note that the is marked 'Overse Shipper' on the si (SCHSM & NG)

ht: Commander-in-
ef of the Army,
~~sident~~ Harry S.
~~man,~~ salutes the
~~ours~~ as he reviews the
~~ssed~~ ranks of the 2d
~~nored~~ Division, in
~~in,~~ July 1945. Known
~~Hell~~ on Wheels', this
the division formerly
~~nmanded~~ by General
~~on~~ himself between
~~uary~~ 1941 and
~~ruary~~ 1942. Note that
M3 half-track has been
~~d~~ with additional
~~d-rails~~ for use by the
~~s.~~ (SCHSM & NG)

ht: In place of reindeer,
~~ep~~ escorts 'St.
~~holas'~~ to a Christmas
~~ty~~ for the children of
~~rz,~~ Luxembourg. The
~~ly~~ versatile and
~~oved~~ jeep was one of
most widely used
~~icles~~ of the war. Of
~~cial~~ interest is the wire
~~er~~ attached to the
~~nt~~ of the jeep. This was
~~eld~~ modification that
designed to snap wire
~~t~~ had been slung across
~~ds~~ as an anti-personnel
~~ice.~~ Visible in the
~~kground~~ are three
~~bulances.~~ (SCHSM &

Left: A dog is a man's best friend. This Germ[an] dog has befriended a member of the 26th Infantry Division. The [man] is armed with an M1 ca[r]bine. Just visible is his right hand on which h[e is] wearing an olive drab (OD) wool leather-palm[ed] glove. These gloves we[re] made of blanket-weigh[t] wool and had a leather palm sewn to the insi[de]. Around his neck he is wearing a Red Cross manufactured scarf. T[he] local Red Cross chapte[rs] throughout America k[nit]ted scarves, sweaters a[nd] socks for troops in the field. They were knitte[d] in OD wool and would have had a tag, bearing the name of the chapt[er] that had knitted the ite[m] sewn to it. (SCHSM & M[...])

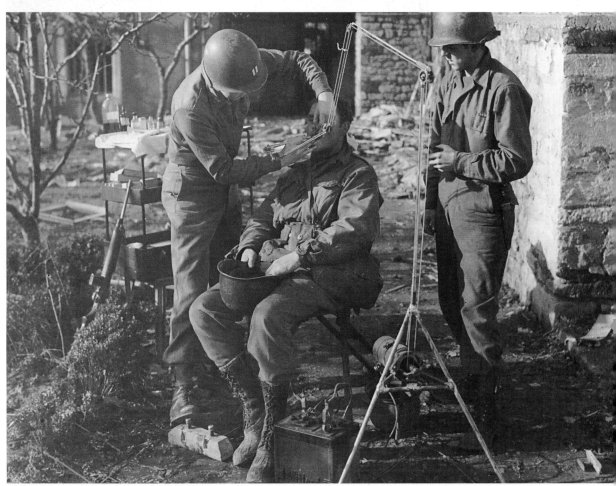

[Top right]: Somewhere in France, a [sol]dier takes advantage of a [brea]k in the Allied advance to [clea]n up. The man is wearing a [five-]button high neck sweater. [He h]as removed the liner from [his] M1 helmet and used the [shel]l as a wash basin. The M1 [hel]met was one of the most [prac]tical items of equipment [issu]ed to the GI in Europe. The [hel]met was used for a variety of [fun]ctions that the helmets [des]igners had not originally [inte]nded. (SCHSM & NG)

[Cen]tre right: George Lithicum, [lef]t, and a friend, relax in a [rece]ntly liberated town. Along [with] 'liberated' beaver-skin [hats], both men wear the stan-[dard] issue wool flannel shirt [and] mustard trousers. Lithicum [app]ears to be wearing a sweater [und]erneath his shirt. (SCHSM &

[Bott]om right: Soldiers of the [317]th Infantry Regiment, 80th [Infa]ntry Division, pause for a [snap]shot prior to embarking for [hom]e leave in the United States. [Sma]ll numbers of soldiers who [had] seen significant periods of [serv]ice were granted home [leav]e during the war. These [men] wear a combination of M41 [and] M43 field jackets and two-[buc]kle combat boots. The man [seat]ed fourth from the left has [a G]erman pistol attached to his [belt]. (SCNA)

[Left]: A dental unit does its job [not] far from the front lines. The [dril]l is powered by a German [car] battery. The patient is wear-[ing] the 12-inch shoe-pacs. [The]se boots had rubber bot-[tom]s and leather uppers. A sol-[dier] would have considered [him]self to be fortunate to have [obt]ained a pair. The dentist [ope]rating on the left is wearing [the] standard wool uniform and [two-]buckle combat boots. His [shir]t is the officers' model. [Offi]cers' shirts had two [epa]ulets, while enlisted shirts [did] not. (SCNA)

Left: Major General J.S. Wood, commander of the 4th Armored Division, standing on the right, prepares to christen his new jeep 'Mary Lou IV'. Gener Wood is wearing a British made ETO jacket and par trooper jump boots. (SCN

Left: A long-service mast sergeant in the 5th Infant Division is congratulated well-wishers prior to his return to the United State in 1944. He is wearing th M1939 wool service jacke This jacket, originally designed as a field garme was worn strictly as a dre or Class A, jacket during war. On the left shoulder from top to bottom are th 5th Infantry Division sho der patch, master sergear stripes, overseas stripes f service in both World Wa and World War II and ser chevrons. Each diagonal stripe represents three ye of service. (SCNA)

Left: A signal corps soldi operates a portable field telephone exchange. This exchange could keep a cc mander in touch with sev al of his positions at one time. The operator wears the five-button high neck sweater and wool trouser (SCNA)

Right: Two headquarters men work on one of the mountains of paperwork required to keep Patton's Army moving. The man on the left wears a newly issued field jacket. The staff sergeant on the right wears an M41 field jacket and mustard trousers with double-buckle combat boots. The sergeant appears to have added hobnails to the bottom of his boots. This was seldom seen on these boots as they were issued with rubber soles. (SCNA)

Right: An ordnance specialist works on a Browning .50 calibre machine gun. He is wearing the jeep cap and herringbone twill (HBT) fatigue jacket. After the summer of 1944, HBTs were more frequently found on rear-echelon troops. The sleeve that has been placed on this .50 calibre indicates that it would be mounted on a vehicle. This heavy machine gun had a rate of fire from 450 to 575 rounds per minute and was mounted on a wide variety of armoured and soft-skinned vehicles. (SCNA)

Left: An officer re[ads?] the articles of wa[r] [to?] his men. The offi[cer is?] wearing an M43 f[ield] jacket. He has slu[ng?] an M4 gas mask b[ag?] over his left shou[lder.] He is not wearing [his?] rank on his jacke[t and?] has not painted t[he?] vertical white stri[pe,] used to signify of[fi-] cers, on the back [of?] his helmet. The m[en?] standing around [him?] are wearing M41 f[ield] jackets. The soldi[er?] just to the officer['s?] right has found a [?] winter combat he[lmet?] and is wearing it [?] under his helmet [for?] added warmth. Vi[sible?] at the top of the p[ic-] ture, standing on [a?] wall, is a man wea[ring?] the first pattern m[ack-] inaw. The first pa[ttern?] can be identified [by?] the wool shawl co[llar.] Later models of t[his?] jacket had a cotto[n?] collar. (SCNA)

Right: A young soldier of the 8th Infantry Division poses for a formal portrait. He is wearing the M1939 wool service jacket over a cotton khaki service shirt and tie. The khaki cotton shirt was often worn with the service jacket in place of the more uncomfortable wool shirt. This soldier has been assigned to an infantry regiment; this can be determined by the crossed rifles on the collar disk on his left lapel. The 8th Infantry Division patch, a blue shield with a white figure eight and a gold arrow going through the number, is sewn to his left shoulder. The fact that there are no campaign ribbons or qualification badges on his jacket would indicate that he has yet to be assigned to the front lines. (Author)

Right: A typical rifleman of the Third Army. The soldier is armed with the .30 calibre M1 Garand rifle, the standard rifle for all G.I.s during World War II called by Patton 'the greatest battle implement ever devised'. He is wearing an M43 field jacket with wool shirt and five-button sweater. He has a late pattern helmet net over his helmet. To his load bearing equipment he has attached an MkA1 fragmentation grenade. (SCNA)

Left: Three 5th Infantry Division medics are sorting through clothes left at a battlefield clearance centre. They all have the 5th Division insignia, a red diamond, sewn to their left shoulders. Of special interest are their helmets. At the centre of the red cross on the front of their helmets they have painted the divisional insignia inside a white circle. The soldier on the left is holding up an M1939 overcoat. This overcoat was not favoured for field use as it became heavy when wet. However, during the extreme cold of the winter of 1944–45, many soldiers wore these for added warmth. The soldier on the right is holding a pair of the rough-out service shoes. The service shoe was the standard footwear for much of the war but was gradually replaced by the two-buckle combat boot.

Left: Private Lloyd Spencer, left, and Private Bryson, right of the 104th Infantry Regiment, take a break from the fighting in Luxembourg. Private Spencer has been able to obtain a winter combat jacket which he wears inside the winter overalls. On his feet he wears arctic overshoes. Private Bryson wears the M1939 overcoat. Bryson wears a hood fashioned from blanket material and the leather palmed OD gloves. Also of interest are the two types of rifle slings in use. Spencer has the earlier M1907 leather model, while Bryson uses the M1 web version. The web sling was introduced later in the war to conserve leather.

Left: Corporal Carlton Chapman, an M4 Sherman tank machine gunner in the 761st Tank Battalion. This picture was taken while the 761st was supporting the famed 'Red Ball Express', a truck convoy system that delivered badly needed fuel and supplies to Patton's rapidly advancing armoured columns. Chapman is wearing the winter combat jacket. He also is wearing the standard M1 helmet in place a tanker's helmet. Just visible on the top of the hatch is an M3 'Greasegun'. This weapon was standard issue to tank crews as its compact size allowed it to be stored inside the tank. (SCAPA)

bbacco was one of the principal forms of relief available to soldiers in the ETO. Here, a grizzled veteran enjoys a cigar. He is wearing the wool knit beanie cap and an M41 field jacket. He has rolled the sleeves of his field jacket back to shorten em, revealing the jacket's lining. This was often required as the field jacket sleeves tended to be too long and loose at the cuff. Underneath his jacket he is wearing the five-button high neck sweater and wool field shirt. (SCNA)

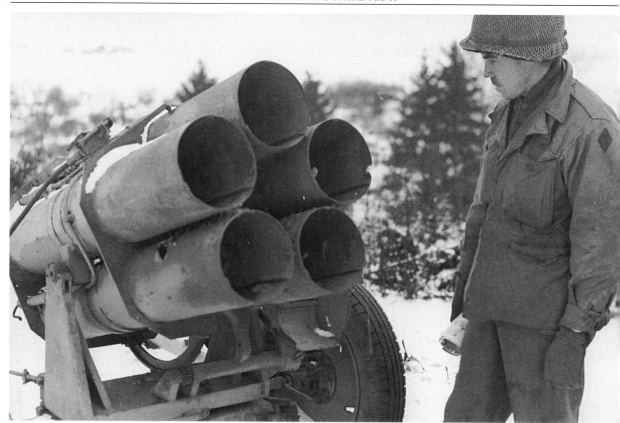

...osite page, top: A soldier of the 5th Infantry Division takes a look at ...man Nebelwerfer rocket launcher. The photograph gives a detailed ...at the M1943 field jacket, late war helmet net, wool and leather ...s and canvas and rubber overshoes. His 5th Infantry Division patch ...scaped the censor's scrutiny and can still be seen on this picture. ...PA)

...osite page, bottom: Corporal Charles Naska, left, and Sergeant ...n Harshman, of the 501st Ordnance Maintenance Company, work ...e electrical system of a bazooka. Around them are spread a variety ...apons that they will refurbish for use by front line soldiers. Leaning ...st the table in front of them can be seen a later model M9 folding ...oka, the barrels of two .50 calibre machine guns and a carbine. On ...ight of the picture can be seen a stack of M3 'Greasegun' sub- ...ine guns and stocks for M1 Garand rifles. Harshman has sewn the ...l Army patch to the left shoulder of his field jacket. (SCHSM & NG)

...ve: In 1945 a soldier inspects a recently captured German flak posi- ...He is wearing the winter combat 'tanker's' jacket and wool trousers. ...rousers are the later pattern that were introduced with the other ...pattern uniforms and equipment. These later trousers were browner ...ade than the earlier mustard trousers, and featured a flap closure on ...ip pocket. (SCA)

...t: Although never used in combat, such was the fear of enemy use ...ison gas that every soldier was issued a gas mask and expected to ...w how it functioned. Here, a soldier is emerging from a gas chamber ...gned to test the mask and the soldiers skill in using one. The soldier ...aring an M4 gas mask. While many soldiers threw away their masks, ...t kept the haversack that the mask came in to carry additional ...onal items.

Left: A soldier ex
ines a shell from
of the dreaded
German Nebelwe.
'screaming meem
mortars. He is we
an M41 field jack
wool shirt and fiv
button sweater.
Around his neck
has improvised a
danna to decreas
chafing that the v
shirt, which was
unlined, common
caused to the nec
(SCA)

Left: Sergeant
Lawrence Gewtting
the 320th Infantry
Regiment, 35th
Infantry Division,
the skies for the m
needed air support
Gewttings is eating
can of C rations th
has heated on a sn
portable stove. He
wearing the first
pattern, all rubber,
arctic overshoes. T
had largely been
replaced by canvas
rubber overshoes t
this point in the wa
He is armed with a
calibre M1 carbine.
visible behind
Gewtting's foxhole
portable field phon
(SCHSM & NG)

Above: Three soldiers of the 28th Division line up at an awards ceremony in Germany. The men on the left and the right both wear the arctic field jacket. Although similar to the 1941 field jacket, the arctic field jacket was longer in the waist and was lined with blanket weight material. The soldier on the right has been able to use a pair of medics' suspenders to support his pistol belt. These suspenders were specially designed to carry aid-bags, and were not meant to be used by infantrymen. Also of interest is the helmet of the man in the centre. The divisional patch has been painted to the front of the helmet. (HSM & NG)

Right: Next to food, mail was one of the highest priorities for sustaining the troop's morale. Here, a soldier wearing an M41 field jacket is sealing a V-Mail letter to the folks back home. This letter would be photographed and microfilmed. The film would then be sent to the States where it would be copied onto a smaller form and delivered to the recipient. Although this system required short letters, it did ensure that the huge volume of mail could continue to be shipped back and forth from the United States and Europe without overwhelming the Army's ability to ship it. (SCNA)

Above: A 90th Infantry Division M1A1 bazoo
crew strike a pose for the camera in 1944. T
man on the left is wearing an M41 field jacke
and mustard trousers. He is the team's loade
and is holding the mortar's rocket. The gunn
centre, is wearing HBT trousers and a wool
shirt. (SCNA)

Left: A gunner of a 155mm howitzer loads th
powder charge that was required to propel th
95-pound shell to ranges of up to 16,000 yar
He is wearing an M41 field jacket and M1 hel
met. The photograph clearly illustrates the
leather chin strap over the brim of the helme
(SCNA)

t: George Lithicum of the 26th Infantry
sion Reconnaissance Detachment is wearing
winter combat uniform and M1 helmet dur-
he drive to relieve Bastogne. He is wearing
rctic overshoes and has armed himself with
 calibre M1 Garand rifle. The eight shot,
-automatic, Garand was the standard fire-
 of the G.I. during World War II and
inued in use through the Korean War.
ISM & NG)

w: At the end of the war, a Third Army and
sian MP work together in Austria directing
fic. The American MP is wearing the stand-
wool shirt and trousers. He has dressed up
appearance somewhat with the painted
net liner and white gloves, although he does
 wear a white pistol belt, which would have
e with the MP's equipment on more formal
y. Visible across his chest is the sling for the
calibre carbine. (SCA)

Above: A group of soldiers from the 320th Infantry Regiment, 35th Infantry Division, t warm themselves during the fight to relieve Bastogne. The men have adopted a variety measures to combat the cold. The two men the right are wearing wool overcoats, the m third from the left appears to have placed h M43 jacket's detachable hood under his hel The three men sitting on the left are wearin M43 jackets over M41 jackets, wool shirts a thermal tops. (SCHSM & NG)

Left: Weary combat veterans enjoy a hot me This photograph is a good illustration of th appearance of fighting men just behind the front lines. The soldier on the left is wearin overcoat over a 43 field jacket and five-butt sweater. On his feet he wears the earlier, all ber, arctic overshoes. He also has removed web chin strap from the bales of his helmet was more common to buckle these straps to back of the helmet. The men are using a jee trailer, covered in a tarpaulin, as a dining ta (SCHSM & NG)

Right: Vehicle crewmen prepare a meal from second half of a ten-in-one ration. This ratic was designed to feed ten men for one day. was a favourite of soldiers for the variety it offered over the more common C and K rati However, due to its size, it was seldom used infantrymen. It was more commonly carried consumed by vehicle crews and those fortu enough to be in one position for a prolonge period of time. (SCNA)

Left: During the Battle of the Bulge these infantryman line up for a hot meal. All of the men are wearing the rubber and canvas overshoes. The man standing third from the left has an M1 Garand M1 cleaning kit attached to his rifle. This cleaning kit would have been shared amongst the members of his squad and was intended to supplement the cleaning equipment that each soldier carried. Many of the men in this picture have improvised hoods out of blankets to wear under their helmets. (NA)

Above: An artilleryman takes a break to have a quick meal. Just visible on his table of shell cases is the issue fork. The hole was placed in the fork so that it could be slid over the handle of the mess kit to aid in cleaning. The diner is wearing a jeep cap and an arctic field jacket. The arctic field jacket was similar to the M41 jacket but was cut longer in the waist and lined with heavier wool. Although it had been cl_ sified as limited standard by 1944, and should not have been issued in the field, the shortage of winter clothing a_ the severity of the winter necessitated that thousands of these jackets be issued. (SCNA)

Left; Two tankers of the 4th Armored Division enjoy a break in the act_ The sergeant on the left wearing the armored forces' helmet. This hel_ was designed to lessen _ impact of blows receive_ while riding inside a moving vehicle and offered no ballistic pro_ tion. Often, tankers wou_ wear the shell of the M1 helmet over this piece o_ headgear for added pro_ tion. The man on the rig_ is drinking from a Worl_ War I vintage canteen c_ The early date of this cu_ can be determined from the rolled edge. It was found that the rolled ed_ became too hot to hold the mouth when drinkir_ hot liquid and later ver_ sions of this cup were stamped and did not ha_ the rolled edge. (SCNA)

ht: Thomas O'Brien tries to enjoy a hot meal.
rien has draped a blanket over his mackinaw
ket. Under his helmet he is wearing the wool
tective hood. This hood was designed to be worn
toned to the back of the shirt. The hood, treated
h an anti-chemical agent that made it sticky to the
ch, was issued during the winter of 1944–45 as a
ogap measure. He is eating out of an M1932 mess
Earlier mess kits did not have the divided lid
tion that O'Brien has laid in the snow. Also at his
t is the M1910 cup. The canteen slid into this cup,
l both units were carried in the canteen carrier
iched to the belt. O'Brien's cup is the earlier
sion with the rolled edge. (SCA)

ow: American soldiers generated a great deal of
erest from Europeans wherever they went. Not
y were they the liberators who had travelled so far
ree them from German occupation, but they came
m a country legendary for its wealth and
indance. Here recently liberated civilians look on
iously as a group of G.I.s prepare a meal. The men
all wearing the wool uniform with leggings. The
n seated at the right is wearing the M43 field
ket. The two men in the the centre are wearing the
lier pattern service shoe, identified by the toe-cap
the boot. (SCNA)

Opposite page, top:
During the advance to Bastogne, members of the 2d Cavalry Group read about their exploits in *Stars and Stripes*, the G.I. newspaper. *Stars and Stripes* was written entirely by G.I.s, for G.I.s, and, much to the consternation of many senior officers, was not subject to rigid supervision by higher authority. They are all wearing the winter combat uniform. Just visible on the man standing third from the left is a grenade ring that this tanker has attached to the zip of his jacket. He is wearing the rubber all-purpose goggles on his helmet. The man seated on the right is wearing the winter combat helmet for added warmth. This would be worn underneath the tanker's helmet. The two soldiers pointing are both wearing gloves made of blanket wool with leather palms. (SCNA)

Opposite page, bottom: Soldiers celebrate with a captured German hunting horn. The men on the left and third from the left wear the M43 field jacket, while the man in the centre and the one on the extreme right wear the winter combat jacket. The man on the right is also wearing the wool knit mechanic's cap which had no brim. Both of these caps were supposed to be worn only under the helmet for additional comfort and warmth.

Above: Soldiers celebrate the liberation of a French village in 1944. The soldier standing on the left is wearing the wool shirt and second pattern herringbone twill fatigue pants. He has stuffed his M1911A1 .45 calibre pistol into a pistol belt instead of the leather holster. Around his neck he has fashioned a scarf made from camouflage parachute material.

Above: As the saying goes, there are no atheists in foxholes. These soldiers attend a religious service in the field. The minister is wearing Army issue religious raiments. Behind him, on the hood of his jeep, the minister has an issue communion kit. The congregation seated around him are wearing a variety of wool and HBT uniforms. The man kneeling third from the right is wearing the second model HBT trousers. These trousers featured large patch pockets on each thigh. The soldier seated seventh from the left is wearing an overseas cap with light blue (infantry) branch of service piping. Overseas caps were not often worn in the field. (SCA)

Left: This group of G.I.s being shipped to Europe in the hold of troop ship are just a few of the millions of men who were sent overseas. The man reading the magazine is wearing the M41 field jacket, while the men at the top and second from the bottom have stripped down to their wool shirts. The soldiers at the top and the bottom are wearing the A4 mechanics' cap without a visor, while the man second from the bottom wears the more common 'jeep cap', hated by senior officers and loved by the men throughout the war. (SCAPA)

Left: High point men of the 2nd Armored Division pass the time while waiting to be shipped home. Points were awarded for time spent overseas, decorations etc. Those with the highest number of points would be shipped home first. Although the 2nd Armored Division did not serve in the Third Army, Patton had commanded the 2nd shortly after its creation. Five of the six are wearing 'Ike' jackets, while the man at left wears the winter combat jacket. The man on the right has an overseas cap with branch piping. The man on the left wears the later pattern overseas cap with no piping. (SCA)

Right: An M4A3 Sherman tank of the 761st Tank Battalion near Nancy, France, in November 1944. The 761st was an African-American tank battalion that earned great distinction during the Northwest Europe campaign while serving in the Third Army. Of special interest, these tankers all wear the M1 helmet for added ballistic protection instead of the tanker's helmet. The tanker at the front left of the turret has armed himself with an M3 'Greasegun', to protect the tank from enemy infantrymen. (NAPA)

Above: Outside Bastogne, tankers of the 6th Armored Division change the tracks on a tank. This laborious and time consuming process was despised by tankers. The men are wearing the standard winter combat uniform with M1 hel- mets. They have whitewashed their M4 Sherman tank for extra protection. The two plates welded to the right side of the tank were added to areas near ammunition storage poi within the tank for added ballistic protection. (SCAPA)

above: A tank commander wearing the winter combat uniform with the jacket worn inside the overalls for added warmth. He is scanning the area around his vehicle with the standard issue M3 binoculars that he has secured with an improvised neck strap. He is wearing an M1 helmet. At his side is the vehicle's .50 calibre machine gun. This gun would have provided anti-aircraft protection and would have been effective against ground targets as well.

Below: Tanks require constant maintenance if they are to continue operating. Here, a technician 5th grade of the 6th Armored Division checks on his tank's treads. The treads have had 'cleats' added to improve traction. The tanker is wearing a standard M1 helmet instead of the tanker's helmet. He is also wearing the winter combat jacket and trousers. The winter combat jacket, often called the 'tanker's jacket' was highly prized by both infantrymen and tankers throughout the war. An infantry soldier who had obtained one of these jackets would have considered himself very lucky. (SCA)

opposite page, bottom: First Lieutenant Ode ns listens to commu- tions on the radio of erman tank. Odens is ring the officers' l overcoat and the oured force's helmet. ANH-1 headset ivers would be ched to ear pieces de the helmet. He is ling in his hand a from the tank that ld be attached to the net so that he could n to radio traffic. tank he is resting on been camouflaged a combination of t and sheets. (SCA)

Above: A Third Army tank destroyer crew enjoys a card game before continuing the advance into Germany. This photograph illustrates the tremendous amount of extra equipment that vehicle crews would carry. Attached to the back of their tank destroyer are two army duffle bags, a frying pan and a box of ten-in-one rations. Also visible, on the rear left of the tank destroyer, is a German mess kit.

Opposite page, bottom: Gunners of Battery C, 398th Armored Field Artillery Battalion, 8th Armored Division, prepare to fire on enemy positions in Germany. Two of these men have whitewashed their helmets for camoufla protection. The two men on the left have been able to obtain armoured forces' winter combat helmets for adde warmth under their helmets. This photograph is a good illustration of the interior of the 105mm, M7 self-propell gun. (SCA)

Above: An M32B1 tank recovery vehicle from the 6th Armored Division during a break in the advance through Belgium. The M32 would be used to extricate damaged tanks from the battlefield. It was mounted on an M4 Sherman chassis. The turret was fixed in place and it removed damaged vehicles with the help of a 60,000-pound winch. The 6th Armored Division designation can just be seen on the front left of the vehicle. (SCAPA)

Above: A 6th Armored Division M7 self-propelled artillery piece named 'All American' takes up its firing position. The M7 featured a 105mm howitzer mounted onto a Sherman tank chassis. In addition to its howitzer, the M7 was armed with a .50 calibre machine gun for defence. The crew of '. American' have secured several logs to the side of their v cle; these would be used to assist the crew in getting free soft ground if they became stuck in the mud. (SCNA)

Left: 101st Airborn artillerymen constr a shelter out of use ration boxes during the battle of the Bu Although he did nc normally command any airborne units, Patton did commar the 101st for a sho time during the Ardennes offensive These men are not wearing anything t would set them ap as airborne soldier and appear just as regular infantryme the Third Army did this time.

ht: The crew of a 5mm 'Long Tom' hower prepares to fire on emy positions. The men ramming a round into chamber of the gun. Of cial interest is the camlage netting which the w has draped over the . These nets were issued variety of sizes to llery and vehicle crews. nets were designed to ceal the positions from my aircraft and ground ervation. The cardboard e laying just outside of gun position was used ransport rounds for the e. (SCA)

ht: Gunners prepare to another round into a mm gun. The man in centre is wearing the field jacket and tard trousers. Visible er his jacket are the button high neck ter, wool shirt and underwear top. The with the cigarette in mouth is wearing a first ern HBT jacket over his r clothing. The first el HBT jacket can be nguished by the waist with pull tab and two ns at the bottom of acket. (SCNA)

t: A self-propelled m 'Long Tom' hownamed 'Aiming Circle e', fires on German ions. The soldier ling at the left has just d the lanyard on the The self-propelled 155 nounted on an M4 nan tank chassis. Of al interest is the blade e rear of the vehicle. was lowered when the e arrived in its posi-As the gun was fired, ade would dig into ound and prevent the om being forced out sition. (SCA)

Left: An M8 armou[]
car of the 26th Infa[]
Division reconn-
aissance troop. The[]
photograph gives a[]
clear view of some[]
the extensive field
modifications that
would transform m[]
vehicles in Europe []
function better in c[]
bat. This armoured
has had an additio[]
stowage rack adde[]
the back. The crew
have attached their
M36 musette bags []
this stowage rack. (
SM & NG)

Left: A Willys jeep
the 26th Infantry
Division recon-
naissance troop. T[]
jeep is equipped w[]
a .30 calibre machi[]
gun mounted to th[]
front right of the j[]
On the left side is []
leather scabbard t[]
was used to carry []
Thompson sub-
machine gun or M[]
Garand. The rear o[]
this jeep has been
modified in the fie[]
with the addition []
stowage rack that []
tains additional su[]
plies for the crew.
(GLHSM & NG)

Left: M8 armoured
cars of the 26th
Infantry Division b[]
worked on by their
crews. The M8 was
principal armoure[]
car of the Army du[]
the final campaign
Europe. It was arm[]
with a 37mm gun.
(GLHSM & NG)

ve: A vehicle crewman assists medics to evacuate the
nded. The crewman is wearing the standard winter com-
uniform with an improvised holster to which he has
ched a bayonet. The medic sitting in the jeep wears the
l, and final, pattern mackinaw jacket that featured a
hed collar. The jeep has been modified by the addition
rackets at the front, centre and rear. Stretchers would be
red to these brackets so that wounded soldiers could be
uated more quickly.

Below: A jeep of the 1st Battalion, 104th Infantry Regiment,
26th Infantry Division, moves through Esch-sur-Sûre,
Luxembourg, prior to an attack on Wiltz, Luxembourg. The
unit's designation can be clearly seen on the left side of the
jeep's bumper. Just visible on the passenger side hood of the
vehicle is a machine-gun mount for a .30 calibre machine gun.
Veterans of the 26th Division have stated that during the Battle
of the Bulge, one way to tell friend from foe was for every man
in the division to wear their gas mask bags as pictured by the
man walking up the road on the right. (SCNA)

Left: A crewman of a[ ]
M3 halftrack washes [ ]
vehicle's mascot. The
rubber tread of the M[ ]
tracks is visible on th[ ]
right hand side of the
picture. The soldier is
wearing the third pat[ ]
HBT trousers and sec[ ]
pattern top. The seco[ ]
pattern jacket can be
distinguished by its p[ ]
patch pockets, the
trousers can be ident[ ]
fied as third pattern [ ]
the bellows pocket o[ ]
the left thigh and the
plastic button which [ ]
a feature of late prod[ ]
tion HBT trousers. He
wearing the standard
helmet. The elastic ba[ ]
(issued with the net)
around the outside
indicates the helmet [ ]
is a late issue. (SCNA)

Left: 35th 'Santa Fe'
Infantry Division sold[ ]
cross a river in Franc[ ]
The bridge they are
crossing has only
recently been comple[ ]
by the engineer soldi[ ]
who are looking on. T[ ]
lead vehicle is a weap[ ]
carrier assigned to th[ ]
134th Infantry Regim[ ]
35th Division. The un[ ]
designation can be
identified on the left
edge of the bumper. [ ]
number on the extrem[ ]
left is for division, th[ ]
regiment. Armoured
divisions would have
a triangle after the
number on the bump[ ]
(SCHSM & NG)

A bulldozer of the 243d Engineer Battalion fills in shell s at the conclusion of the battle for St Vith. Bulldozers a as this would have been an Army level asset, and would e been assigned to specific divisions on an as needed s. (SCA)

Above: An African-American artillery unit hauls its 105mm howitzer to new positions outside Bastogne in December 1944. They are hauling their gun with a Mack truck. This was acommon vehicle in Patton's Third Army throughout the war in Europe and was used in a wide range of capacities. It was the primary vehicle used in the 'Red Ball Express'. (SCAPA)

Left: Three members of the 101(st?)
Engineers, are being relieved aft(er)
holding positions throughout a (very?)
cold evening in 1945. Two of the(se men)
are armed with bazookas. The m(an in)
the front is wearing a wool over(coat)
over his other clothing. His divis(ion)
patch has been sewn to the left
shoulder. The man on the left is
wearing the OD wool protective
(SCA)

Below: Soldiers of the 48th Arm(ored)
Infantry Battalion, 7th Armored
Division, on a patrol in St Vith. A(ll)
the men are wearing a snow suit (of)
some sort. All four suits appear (to be)
well constructed garments and (not?)
just improvised. The men are tra(vel-)
ling very light and carry only ba(n-)
doleers for their M1 rifles. (SCA)

t: During the winter of 1944–45, y G.I.s discovered the desirability aving some kind of snow camou- e to wear during the winter. While U.S. Army did have some snow ouflage clothing, its presence on front lines in Europe was very rare. e often than not, commanders d contract with local European s or civilians to make uniforms, or iers would improvise with locally ined white linens. These men ear to have improvised ponchos helmet covers out of linen table- hs and sheets. (SCA)

w: Men from Company C, 23rd ored Infantry Battalion, 7th ored Division, look for snipers in ith, Belgium, in January 1945. Most ese men are wearing improvised v camouflage over their uniforms. two men squatting second from left and in the centre appear to be ring prefabricated snow suits. The rman tank crewman in the back- und has not made any attempt at ouflaging himself although he has that his M4A3 tank received a coat hitewash. (SCA)

Above: Machine gunners of the 104th Infantry Regiment, 4th Armored Division, wait for an M4 Sherman tank to move against enemy positions during the 4th Armored's advance to Bastogne. The gunners are equipped with the M1911A1 .30 calibre machine gun. The infantryman on the left wears the M43 field jacket, while the machine gunner on the right is still wearing the earlier M41 field jacket. (SCAPA)

Below: Private John McFarlane and Lloyd Lockwood of the 35th Infantry Division man an M1917A1 .30 calibre machine gun east of Bastogne. The M1917A1 was the air cooled version of this machine gun. These machine gunners have spread wool blankets over their foxholes for added warmth (SCAPA)

w: A column of well laden G.I.s advance down a fire break
Belgian forest. All of these men are wearing their over-
s and carry the jungle pack. Due to the extremely cold
ditions, and frozen ground, these men all appear to have
arded their shovels. These would normally be attached to
back of the pack. One veteran of the battle of the Bulge
lled that due to the frozen ground, entrenching tools were
thless for preparing positions. In these conditions, many
iers had to rely on small amounts of explosives to blast
ting positions into the ground. (SCHSM & NG)

Bottom: Armoured infantrymen of the 7th Armored Division
move past a destroyed German self-propelled gun. Most of
the men are wearing a camouflaged helmet cover of some
sort over their helmets. They are also carrying well stuffed
M1928 haversacks. The man marching fourth from the left is
using a rifle to support an extra blanket. The man marching
at the rear is wearing an Army Air Force fleece lined jacket.
The fact that this man is not carrying any equipment or
weapon would indicate that he is not a member of this
infantry unit. (SCA)

Above: A bazooka crew prepare to fire on a target. The man at the right is loading an M6A1 round into the back of the bazooka. Spare rounds are carried in the tubes on the ground in front of the loader. Both men are wearing M43 field jackets with attached hoods. These hoods were infrequently seen in the ETO. The loader has also improvised some sort of helmet cover for his M1 helmet. (SCNA)

Right: A machine-gun crew of I Company, 3rd Battalion, 242nd Infantry Regiment, 42nd Infantry Division, prepares a machine-gun position in eastern France in January 1945. All of the men are wearing the M43 field jackets. The field jacket hood is clearly illustrated by the man standing on the right. The man sitting in the centre is checking the rounds on the cloth ammo belts for his crew's .30 calibre machine gun. (SCHSM & NG)

osite page, top: During the summer of 1944 a 60mm
tar crew is in action in France. The 60mm mortar was
standard light mortar of the American infantryman dur-
World War II. This 42-pound weapon could fire either
explosive or illuminating rounds at targets from 100 to
0 yards away. The soldiers all wear scrim in their helmet
to break up the helmets' profile. (SCHSM & NG)

osite page, bottom: The crew of an 80mm mortar dur-
operations in France. The low trajectory of the mortar,
fact that they have no really prepared position, and that
shells are stacked so close to the gun, would indicate
they are operating at some distance from the front
s. The gunners are wearing second and third pattern

herringbone twill trousers and shirts. The corporal on the
right has sewn his rank insignia to his jacket. This was not a
common practice as the HBT jacket was considered fatigue
clothing. (SCHSM & NG)

Below: Crew of a 4.2-inch mortar in action. The 4.2-inch
mortar was the heaviest calibre of mortar available to
Patton's ground soldiers. These mortars were grouped
together at battalion level and would support infantry and
armoured forces on an as needed basis. Originally intended
to be used in chemical warfare, these mortars instead provided smoke and high explosive support fire to the front line
soldiers. (SCNA)

Above: In 1945, an M1917 .30 calibre machine-gun team takes position in a shell damaged German town. Despite the late date, these men are still armed with the earlier water cooled .30 calibre machine gun. Most units by this point in the war would have been armed with the M1917A1 air cooled .30 calibre machine gun. All three members of the crew wear the M43 jacket. (SCHSM & NG)

Below: During the fighting around Bastogne, machine gunners of the 4th Armored Division protect the flanks of advancing tanks. Both men are wearing overcoats to ward off the cold. The gunner on the right is wearing the later pattern helmet net on his M1 helmet. This can be discerned by the tightness of the mesh and the elastic band around base of the helmet. These nets were issued with an instruction card that explained how the net could be affixed to the helmet with the elastic band on either the outside of the net or underneath it. (SCAPA)

ht: Two muddy
almen of the 87th
sion lay new tele-
ne lines near St
, Belgium. The sol-
on the left is
ring the M1943
l jacket and
sers and the rub-
overshoes. Just
ble on his left leg is
rap for climbing
es. These spikes
ld have been used
elp the signalman
b telephone poles.
man on the right
earing a mackinaw
and M1943 field
sers. He has also
n able to obtain a
r of the 12-inch
e-pacs. (SCA)

ow: In September 1944, an engineer soldier looking
r a destroyed German bunker admires his handiwork.
hough late in the year, the soldier continues to wear
earlier M1941 field jacket and rough-out service shoes
and leggings. He appears just as the first American soldiers in France did in June 1944. He is armed with an M1
Garand rifle and carries a canteen and bayonet attached to
his belt. (SCA)

Above: Engineer soldier prepare to blow up a roa block. The two men in t foreground are wearing the two-buckle combat boots. The photograph illustrates the sole and stitching on these boots The man standing at lef appears to have acquire civilian winter coat of some sort. (SCA)

Left: A soldier of Company C, 66th Armor Infantry Battalion, 12th Armored Division, looks on as a German vehicle burns in the woods near Nuremburg. He is armec with the M1A1 Thomps sub-machine gun. The 1 pound Thompson had a 700-rounds-per-minute rate of fire. This soldier has also obtained a German pistol which he wears on an improvised rig around his waist. (SCHSM & NG)

ve: Soldiers of the 101st Infantry Regiment accept the ender of Fort Jean d'Arc in Metz, France, in December 4. Most of the men are wearing the M43 cotton field et. However, the sergeant at the rear of the column is ring an earlier M41 field jacket. This group of G.I.s is elling light and none of the soldiers is wearing the M28 rsack. Many of the men are wearing the M36 combat enders. (SCHSM & NG)

Below: A machine-gun squad of the 35th Infantry Division advances through a German town. All of the men are wearing the dismounted raincoat over their other clothes. The man at the front is carrying the Browning M1917A1 .30 calibre machine gun. This gun had largely been replaced by the air cooled version of this machine gun by this point in the war. The men marching behind the machine gunner are carrying ammunition for the gun in the cans at their sides. Just visible on the seventh man of the column is the tripod for the gun. (SCHSM & NG)

Above: Soldiers cross a recently built Bailey bridge. These bridges could be constructed rapidly, even under extremely trying conditions, in order to facilitate the continued advance of Patton's men. All of these men have improvised bed rolls that they are using to carry their personal possessions. The soldier on the right of the column wears the olive drab protective hood for additional warmth. Notice the spool of communication wire in the right hand corner of the picture. This spool is being run forward with the troops to link field phones. (SCA)

Below: Soldiers of the 55th Armored Infantry Regiment, 11th Armored Division, advance through a smoking Germ town. Three of the advancing infantryman are wearing th dismounted raincoat underneath their equipment, as is o of the tankers. Also note that both of the tank crewman a wearing standard M1 helmets and not armoured crewme helmets. (SCA)

t: Two MPs direct
c at St Vith. Both
are wearing the
ounted raincoat
arctic overshoes.
are armed with
30 calibre carbine.
MP standing at
as two extra
azines in a pouch
l over the stock.
of interest is the
e stripe on the
et of the MP on
ight.

w: During August 1944, 28th Infantry 'Keystone'
sion military policemen (MPs) search for German snipers
destroyed French town. The MP on the right wears the
and white MP brassard. Brassards were made of wool
were pinned in place. Just above the brassard is the

28th Infantry Division patch. The 28th was originally a
Pennsylvania National Guard division. The division took its
nickname from George Washington's reference to
Pennsylvania as the 'keystone state'. (SCHSM & NG)

A well laden machine gunner dashes for cover. The gunner is carrying the water-cooled .30 calibre machine gun. Over h shoulder he has slung an M3 'Greasegun'. He is wearing an M41 field jacket and wool trousers. Just visible on his left sid the new folding shovel. The folding shovel replaced the earlier T handle shovel in time for the campaign in northwest Europe, and was copied from a German design. (SCHSM & NG)

INDEX